Contents

Introduction

Woods and meadows are places you can visit that are full of all kinds of wildlife. You can have fun playing a game about animal homes. Learn how to draw meadow flowers and look closely at tiny insects. Plant a tree and paint and cut out a camouflaged bird.

1 Look out for numbers like this. They will guide you through the step-by-step instructions for the projects and activities, making sure that you do things in the right order.

Further facts

Whenever you see this 'nature spotters' sign, you will find interesting facts and information, such as where different animals live, to help you understand more about woods and meadows.

discovering nature

Woods and Meadows

Sally Hewitt

Franklin Watts
London • Sydney

An Aladdin Book
© Aladdin Books Ltd 2000
Produced by
Aladdin Books Ltd
28 Percy Street
London W1P OLD

First published in Great Britain
in 2000 by
Franklin Watts Books
96 Leonard Street
London EC2A 4XD

ISBN 0-7496-3716-1 (hardcover)
ISBN 0-7496-4607-1 (paperback)

Editor: Kathy Gemmell

Consultant: Helen Taylor

Designer: Simon Morse

Photography: Roger Vlitos

Illustrators: Tony Kenyon
& Mike Atkinson

Printed in the U.A.E.
A CIP catalogue record for this book
is available from the British Library.

Original design concept by David West Children's Books

Hints and tips

•Try to look at creatures without disturbing them. If you do move them, always return them to the place where you found them.

•Before touching soil or leaves, always cover any cuts with a plaster. Wash your hands afterwards.

•Try not to rub your face or eyes when working with plants or soil.

•Do not touch any fungus and do not pick the flowers.

BE CAREFUL OF STINGING INSECTS

Wherever you see this sign, ask an adult to help you. Never use sharp tools or go exploring on your own.

Get an adult to help you

This special warning sign shows where you have to take particular care when doing the project. For example, when sweeping meadow grasses for insects, be careful of bees and wasps. Don't go too close to them as they may sting you.

Life in a tree

Trees are the biggest plants on Earth. They can live to be very old. All kinds of plants and animals live in the different parts of a tree. Find out which creatures have made their home in a tree near you.

Shake a limb

1 You will need a magnifying glass and a large sheet of card. Lay the card under a low branch of a tree.

2 Shake the branch gently. Look through the magnifying glass at the creatures that fall onto the card. Try to find out what each one is.

Tree creatures

Small creatures can find food in every part of a tree. Sometimes, too many insects can kill a tree.

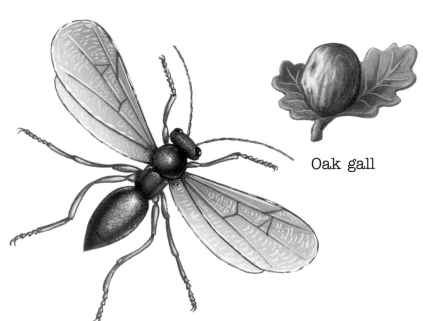

Oak gall

Adult bark beetles feed on buds and new leaves. Their tiny young, called larvae, live in the tree trunk and chew wood.

Gall wasp grubs live inside oak galls. They come out when they have grown into adult gall wasps.

Caterpillars that are the same colour as leaves or twigs can be difficult to spot. Holes in the leaves tell you where they have been feeding.

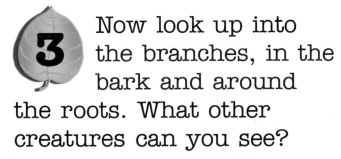

A nut weevil drills a tiny hole and lays its eggs inside a nut such as an acorn. The grubs use the nut for food.

Hole

Acorn

3 Now look up into the branches, in the bark and around the roots. What other creatures can you see?

PUT CREATURES BACK WHERE YOU FOUND THEM

Different woodlands

Trees grow together to form different kinds of woodland. You can tell what kind of woodland you are in by the shape of the leaves. Deciduous trees have wide, flat leaves. Evergreen trees often have tough, shiny leaves.

Sorting and rubbing leaves

1 Try to visit different kinds of woodland. Pick up leaves from the woodland floor.

2 Sort your leaves into piles of different shapes. Use a book to find out which trees they come from. Are they from deciduous or evergreen trees?

3 Make leaf rubbings by laying paper over each leaf, with the rough side of the leaf facing upwards. Rub evenly over the paper with a wax crayon.

Deciduous and evergreen trees

The leaves on deciduous trees change colour then fall off the tree in winter. Evergreen trees keep their leaves all year round. Conifers, such as pine trees, are evergreens. They have long, thin leaves called needles.

Sugar maple   Horse chestnut

Sugar maples and horse chestnuts are deciduous trees.

Scots pine   Holly

Scots pines and holly trees are evergreens. Even evergreen trees will shed a few leaves as new ones grow.

The woodland floor

In deciduous woods in early spring, before leaves have grown on the trees, the floor is filled with light. Evergreen woods are always quite dark because the leaves keep out the light. See what you can find on different woodland floors.

Circle a tree

1 To see what lies under a tree, you can circle it. You will need thick string, twigs, a notebook and a pencil.

2 Press the twigs firmly into the ground around a tree. Loop the string around the twigs to make a circle.

3 Look carefully at the ground inside the string circle. Draw or make a note of what you see.

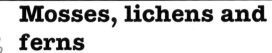

Mosses, lichens and ferns

Mosses, lichens and ferns are all plants that have no flowers. Look out for them growing on a woodland floor.

Lichens grow on stones, trees and soil. They grow very slowly and live for a long time.

Mosses spread over damp ground and on wet logs.

Ferns can grow in many different kinds of soil. Their tightly curled stems open out into green fronds.

DON'T TOUCH DROPPINGS OR FUNGI

4 Use your notes to make a chart of the area under the tree. On a piece of card, draw a circle for the string, then fill in all the things you saw.

Woodland animals

Woodland animals are usually very shy. There are plenty of places to hide in the woods, so they are hard to spot. But you can listen and look for signs that tell you they are not far away.

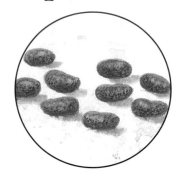

Deer droppings

Spot the signs

1 Look out for deer droppings and footprints. A tree with no low-growing leaves might have had the leaves eaten by a deer. In some places, you can spot where a deer has nibbled a ring of bark from a young tree. This can sometimes kill the tree.

Deer browse (eat) low-growing leaves into a straight line.

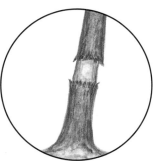

Bark nibbled by deer

2 Badgers look for food at night. They live in holes called setts. See if you can spot bits of plants that they drag into their setts for bedding. Look for badger fur caught on wire.

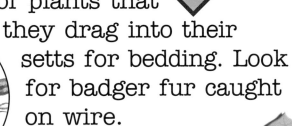

DO NOT TOUCH BARBED WIRE

Squirrel food litter

Squirrel drey

3 Squirrels dart along branches and up and down tree trunks. They build homes called dreys high up in trees. Look under trees for nuts and cones they have dropped.

Hunters and hunted

Foxes and wolves hunt and kill animals that feed on woodland plants. People hunt and eat woodland deer and wild boar.

A red fox has pointed ears and sharp eyes to listen and look for its prey.

A boar is a kind of wild pig. It uses its blunt snout to root for food on the woodland floor.

A wood mouse has sharp teeth for nibbling seeds and nuts. It has to watch out for hungry foxes.

Woodland birds

Woods are good places to look for birds. Walk quietly because sudden noises and movements will frighten them away. In spring, birds build nests in hollow trunks or branches. In summer and autumn, they find insects, seeds, nuts and berries to eat. In winter, they find shelter in the trees.

Cuckoo

1 To find food in winter, cuckoos fly south to warmer places. In spring, they fly back north to breed.

2 The mother cuckoo looks for a nest belonging to another bird. She throws out an egg from the nest, lays one of her own in its place, then flies off.

Sights and sounds

Sometimes it is hard to spot birds through the leaves, especially in darker evergreen woods. Look for flashes of colour as they fly past, and listen for the noises they make.

A woodpigeon makes a soft cooing sound. It hops and flies up in the branches but finds its food on the ground.

Jays are colourful crows and have a harsh cry. They will eat eggs from the nests of smaller birds.

You can hear woodpeckers tapping at tree trunks as they look for insects or drill out a nest hole.

Crossbills live in coniferous forests. They use their crossed bills to pick out the seeds from cones.

3 The cuckoo chick hatches and grows quickly. It pushes the other eggs and smaller chicks out of the nest.

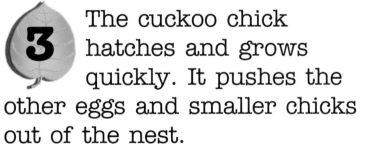

4 The adopted parent birds are kept very busy feeding their big, hungry cuckoo chick.

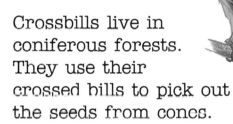

Plant a tree

In the autumn, look out for acorns, conkers and sycamore wings on the woodland floor. They are all different seeds that will grow into new young trees in the spring. Collect some seeds and try to grow trees from them.

See it grow

1 In the spring, push your seeds into the soil, about 2 cm deep. Trees grow very tall, so leave enough room around each one for roots and branches to spread.

2 Make labels and push them into the soil next to the seeds. An acorn will grow into an oak tree and a conker into a horse chestnut tree.

SCOTS PINE

HORSE CHESTNUT

CHESTNUT

OAK

3 Trees grow slowly, so be patient. Some seeds may not grow at all. Make a chart to record the growth of your first shoot.

Tree rings

Each year, a new layer grows around a tree trunk and makes a ring. By counting the rings inside the trunk of a fallen tree, you can tell the tree's age.

It would take a long time to count the rings of giant trees called sequoias — they can live for over a thousand years.

Meadows

Wherever grass is left uncut it grows into a meadow of tall grasses and wild flowers. The green grass becomes golden hay in the summer sun. See for yourself how grass grows back again after it has been cut.

Cut and grow

1 You will need two seed trays filled with soil, a packet of grass seeds, a packet of cress seeds and scissors.

2 Sprinkle grass seeds evenly over the soil in one tray and the cress seeds in the other tray. Put the trays in a sunny place, keep them watered and watch them grow.

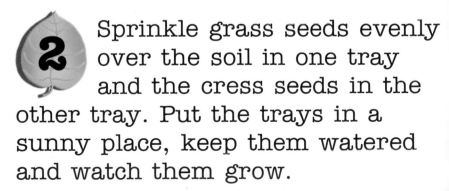

3 When the grass and cress have grown about 3 cm, cut half of each tray. Only the grass will grow back. The cress will only grow again if you plant new seeds.

Harvest

Horses, cows and sheep often graze in meadows. Farmers sometimes harvest the grass in meadows to feed their animals.

Tractors with special mowers cut the grass while it is still green.

A baler machine packs or rolls the grass into bales. The bales are left to dry in the sunshine. The dry grass is called hay.

The hay is stored in dry barns.

In winter, the farmer feeds the animals from the store of hay.

Grasses

The grass in your local park or garden is just one of more than ten thousand different kinds of grasses. Grazing animals like sheep, horses and cows eat grass. But did you know that you eat grass too?

Grasses we eat

1 Wheat, rice, maize and oats are grasses that farmers grow for us to eat. Copy pictures of them onto four pieces of card and label them.

Wheat	Maize	Rice	Oats
A	B	C	D

2 Pour some dry rice, corn kernels (or sweet corn), flour (or wheat grains) and porridge oats into four piles on a piece of card.

Answers:
A = rice
B = wheat grains
C = oats
D = corn kernels

3 Now ask a friend to match each of the four piles to the picture of the crop it came from.

From field to food

All over the world, farmers grow different kinds of grasses for food. These are called cereal crops. The ripe seeds are the grains. They give us some of our most important food.

Wheat is grown in enormous fields. The grains are ground into flour to make bread and pasta.

Rice is grown underwater in paddy fields. We eat cooked rice and grind the grains to make breakfast cereals.

Maize gives us corn on the cob which is good to cook and eat. The grains can be ground into flour.

Oatmeal comes from oats. We use it to make porridge and biscuits.

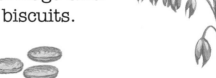

Meadow flowers

In the summer, you can see colourful flowers dotted among the tall meadow grasses. They are bright red, blue, purple and yellow to attract insects. See how many different flowers of each colour you can find in a summer meadow.

Flower sketching

1 To sketch flowers, you will need a sketch book, some coloured pencils and a rubber. Before you start sketching, study the colour of the flowers, how many petals each one has and the shape of their leaves.

Dandelion

Flower

Leaf

Wild flowers

A gardener chooses which flowers to grow in a garden. Meadow flowers grow naturally by spreading their seeds.

The common milkweed grows wild in North America. Soft floss from its seedpods is used for stuffing furniture.

Meadow buttercups have shiny yellow petals. If you hold one under your chin, it makes your skin look yellow like butter.

A thistle has a spiky stem and leaves. Its seeds are on parachutes that blow in the wind.

Look closely at a scabious flower to see that it is made up of a mass of tiny flowers.

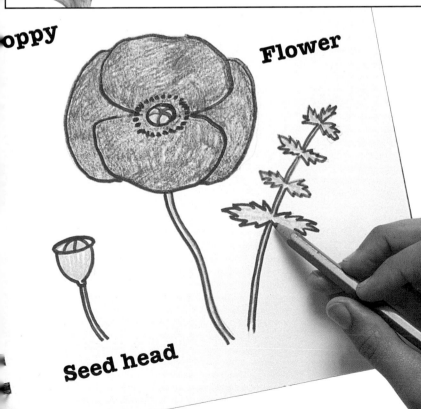

oppy

Flower

Seed head

2 Copy the flowers as carefully and accurately as you can. You can look up any of the ones you don't know in a flower book later.

DO NOT PICK THE FLOWERS

Meadow insects

There are insects all over a meadow. Butterflies fly among the flowers, beetles scuttle along the ground and bugs crawl up stems. Insects too small to spot can be swept up in a net.

Insect sweep

1 To look closely at insects, you will need a net with a long handle, a large sheet of paper and a magnifying glass.

BE CAREFUL OF INSECTS THAT STING

Frog hopper

Horsefly

Lacewing

2 Sweep the net with a long stroke across the top of meadow grasses. Tip out what you have caught onto the paper.

Hoverflies

Brimstone butterfly

Grasshoppers

If you listen carefully, you are sure to hear a grasshopper chirping in a summer meadow. Grasshoppers call to each other either by rubbing their wings together or by rubbing part of their back legs against their wings. They have long, very strong back legs for hopping through the grass.

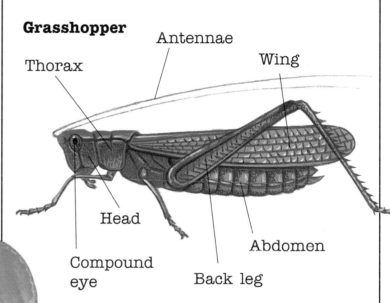

Grasshopper

Antennae

Thorax

Wing

Head

Compound eye

Abdomen

Back leg

A type of grasshopper called a locust is a pest to farmers in many places. Locusts travel in vast swarms and can eat and destroy whole fields of crops.

3 Look carefully at the insects with your magnifying glass. When you have finished, tip them gently back onto the grass.

Meadow birds

Some birds visit meadows to eat seeds, worms, snails and insects. Other birds build their nests there. The colour of their feathers helps them to hide in the grass. This is called camouflage.

Camouflage a bird

1 You will need four big sheets of card, paints and scissors. Paint tall grasses onto one sheet of card.

2 When the paint is dry, draw on a bird shape. Cut it out to leave a bird-shaped hole.

3 Paint the other three pieces of card with different coloured splodges, as shown in the main picture. Use clean water for each colour.

Birds in the grass

You can watch flocks of birds fly in and feed together in meadows all year round.

Canada geese arrive in flocks and graze on the grass. They make a loud, honking noise.

A skylark disguises where its nest is on the ground by landing away from it and then running to it through the grass.

Rooks nest in untidy treetop rookeries. They feed together in meadows eating insects and seeds.

Lapwings sometimes arrive to feed in flocks of thousands. They are sometimes called 'peewits' because of the sound they make.

4 Put each coloured card behind the card with the bird cut out of it. See how some colours camouflage the bird in the grass better than others.

Meadow animals

Grass snakes, moles, rabbits and foxes are all animals you might see in a meadow. They live in holes underground. Animal droppings or fur around a hole may let you know who lives there.

Snake nest

Fox earth

Rabbit warren

Mole nest

Match the homes

1 Draw pictures of a grass snake, a mole, a rabbit and a fox onto four pieces of card. Cut them out.

2 Each animal digs a differently shaped tunnel or hole. Copy pictures of a grass snake nest, a mole nest, a rabbit warren and a fox earth onto four pieces of card.

The harvest mouse

The tiny harvest mouse lives among the grass stalks in fields or meadows.

It hangs onto the stalks with its tail and back legs and uses its front paws to eat the grains.

The mother harvest mouse weaves a round nest made of grass or reed stalks for her babies. In places with hedgerows, she may build a more secure nest by winding stalks of grass around the thicker stalks in the hedge.

3 Hold up each of your tunnel pictures in turn. Ask a friend to match each animal to its home.

Get an adult to help you

Glossary

Camouflage

Camouflage is when the colour and patterns on the coat or feathers of an animal or bird blend in with the background. This makes it hard for an enemy to spot them and helps to keep them safe.

Turn to pages 26-27 to see how to paint and cut out a camouflaged bird.

Cereals

Cereals are types of grasses, such as wheat, oats, rice and maize, which are grown by farmers as crops. Cereals are a very important source of food for people and animals all over the world.

Turn to pages 20-21 to learn about which cereal grasses the food we eat comes from.

Conifers

Conifers are evergreen trees that grow seeds in cones. Pine trees are conifers. They have long, thin leaves called needles.

Find out about conifers on pages 8-9.

Deciduous trees

Deciduous trees have large, flat leaves that change colour in autumn. They lose all their leaves in the winter. In spring, they grow fresh, green leaves.

Learn about deciduous trees on pages 8-9.

Evergreen trees

Evergreen trees are always green because they keep their leaves all year round. Their leaves are often tough and shiny to protect them in cold weather.

Look at evergreen trees on pages 8-9.

Hay

Hay is dried grass. Many animals are fed on hay in the winter when there is no fresh grass.

You can see how hay is prepared and cut on pages 18-19.

Meadow

A meadow is an area where grasses and flowers grow wild. Horses, cows and sheep often graze in meadows. Many different kinds of insects, birds and wild animals make their homes there.

Find out about meadow grasses, flowers, insects, birds and animals on pages 18-29.

Tree rings

Every year, a tree grows a new layer around its trunk, making a tree ring. You can see a tree's rings if you look at the inside of a fallen tree.

You can find out on pages 16-17 how to tell a tree's age by counting its rings.

Woodland

A woodland is a place where trees grow together. A woodland might be made up of mostly evergreen trees, mostly deciduous trees or a mixture of both. Each different woodland has its own special kind of wildlife.

You can find out about the trees and leaves in different woodlands and about the animals and birds that live there on pages 6-17.

Index